UNDERSTANDING
YOUR 5 YEAR-OLD

UNDERSTANDING

YOUR 5 YEAR-OLD

Lesley Holditch

Warwick Publishing
Toronto   Los Angeles

© 1997 Lesley Holditch

All rights reserved. No part of this publication may be reproduced, stored in a retrieval system or data base, or transmitted in any form or by any means, electronic, mechanical, photocopying, recording, or otherwise, without prior permission of the publisher.

ISBN 1-894020-05-7

Published by:
Warwick Publishing Inc., 388 King Street East, Toronto, Ontario M5V 1K2
Warwick Publishing Inc., 1424 N. Highland Avenue, Los Angeles, CA 90027

Distributed by:
Firefly Books Ltd., 3680 Victoria Park Avenue, Willowdale, Ontario M2H 3K1

First published in Great Britain in 1993 by:
Rosendale Press Ltd.
Premier House
10 Greycoat Place
London SW1P 1SB

Design: Diane Farenick

Printed and bound in Canada

CONTENTS

INTRODUCTION 9

CHAPTER 1: YOUR FIVE YEAR-OLD AT SCHOOL 13
The transition from home to school - Preparation for starting school - The world of school - Forming new relationships - The child's experience of school - Integrating the world of home and school - Choosing a school

CHAPTER 2: YOUR FIVE YEAR-OLD AND THE WIDER WORLD . . .27
Religious and cultural differences - The need for rules - Socialization - The games of five year-olds - The discovery of the peer group

CHAPTER 3: INTELLECTUAL DEVELOPMENT 37
Learning to read - The development of mathematical skills - The development of abstract thinking - Language development - Children who have difficulty in learning - Competition: its place in learning - Helping children who have difficulty in learning.

CHAPTER 4: YOUR CHILD IN THE FAMILY 53
Position in the family - The child in relation to the parents - Working parents - Choosing a babysitter - Managing change - The child's place in his family - Looking to the future

FURTHER READING 69

Tavistock Clinic

The Tavistock Clinic, London, was founded in 1920, in order to meet the needs of people whose lives had been disrupted by the First World War. Today, it is still committed to understanding people's needs though, of course, times and people have changed. Now, as well as working with adults and adolescents, the Tavistock Clinic has a large department for children and families. This offers help to parents who are finding the challenging task of bringing up their children daunting and has, therefore, a wide experience of children of all ages. It is firmly committed to early intervention in the inevitable problems that arise as children grow up, and to the view that if difficulties are caught early enough, parents are the best people to help their children with them.

Professional Staff of the Clinic were, therefore, pleased to be able to contribute to this series of books to describe the ordinary development of children, to help in spotting the growing pains and to provide ways that parents might think about their children's growth.

Introduction

"It's my birthday, I'm five years old!" Lucy rushed into her parents' bedroom in great excitement. Suddenly her face fell. "But I don't feel any older than I did yesterday!"

Lucy's disappointment is something that I suspect is familiar to all of us, particularly as a child, when there is a keen wish to grow up. Indeed in James Barrie's well known story of *Peter Pan* he vividly describes the dilemma for Peter Pan, who did not have such a wish, and had therefore to lose Wendy to whom he had become attached, as a prerequisite for the development of this relationship was the necessity to mature and eventually leave the world of childhood behind.

By the age of five children have acquired some degree of independence. They can feed themselves, are toilet trained and have enough language to communicate their needs to an adult. They are also beginning to understand something about the rules of the society they live in, such as the need for adults to work to earn money to live. They are at the stage of beginning to look outwards from the immediate family and will be helped to do this by opportunities to meet other children outside the home. Many children at this age will have the chance to attend a formal group, either a school or a kindergarten.

The five year-old is very much a pragmatist. A sense of reality is still not totally secure so that the stories they enjoy tend to be those depicting situations similar to those they have experienced. Language is developing apace enabling them to converse and ask questions about the environment, in an attempt to make sense of the world around them. They are in the throes of taking the first steps towards finding their identity and discovering how to interact with others.

It could be said that for Lucy, however, her fifth birthday was a particularly important milestone in her life for, like most children her age, it was time to attend regular school. School brings new challenges for five year-olds. They will be faced with a considerable change in life experience. There will now be demands to be more independent, to manage parts of the daily routine alone. For instance it becomes more important to be able to dress without adult help, to fasten shoes or buttons on an outdoor coat. They have to communicate with an unfamiliar adult who will not have the same intimate knowledge of them as a parent. There will be greater demands for independence than at daycare or nursery school. There will be more expectations for the child in school to conform and to participate in a set program or curriculum.

I wonder how many readers of this book can remember the day they started school? Were you looking forward in excited anticipation or were you feeling somewhat apprehensive? If you had a brother or sister already there perhaps you were keen to find out more about their experiences in this unknown world outside home. What was it like to do math and learn to write? Perhaps you have memories of wearing a school uniform which somehow symbolized this new world in a very concrete way. You may have had some notion that at last you would be able to read and write in the same way that adults could.

If you can recall your own experience, what aspect stands out most clearly for you? Is it the feeling of being alone, possibly for the first time without a parent to turn to in times of difficulty, or the bewilderment at being asked to answer "present" when your name was called on the register, although there was no sign of a present to follow? Perhaps the memory that stands out most clearly for you is the feeling of pleasure at the thought of a new and exciting experience?

Whatever your memories contain it is likely that when the time comes for you to take your son or daughter to school for the first time some of those memories will be reactivated and can be of great help to you in your role as a parent. They can enable you to understand the feelings of your child. Sometimes of course, if the memories are unpleasant, it may be necessary to guard against them influencing your judgment in a negative way. It is likely that the school you are taking your child to is different in many ways from the one you remember and you will find that there is a need to adjust your perceptions accordingly.

CHAPTER ONE

Your Five Year-Old At School

The transition from home to school

There are several important transitions in the human life cycle, of which going regularly to school is one. It is perhaps the second major transition in a child's life—the first being weaning. Weaning is a process that usually takes place in the latter part of the first year of life and is a significant move towards independence. The baby begins to eat solid food and gradually gives up the milk produced by Mother. The intimacy and closeness of the feeding relationship prior to weaning is present whether or not the baby is breast fed. Inevitably, then, the baby is made more aware of the separateness that exists between self and mother. This is an important stage in the process of the developing independence of the baby. Each of these transitions, weaning and starting school, is a step on the road to maturity and is a time when the child takes a big step forward.

A transition implies both a beginning and an ending and one would therefore expect to feel some sadness for the loss of what has gone as well as hope and pleasure at a new beginning.

It may perhaps seem surprising that a child who is evidently striving constantly to grow up and is encouraged to do so should also regret the passing of babyhood, but most parents will be familiar with their child reverting to more babyish behavior at times—for instance, when they have become overexcited or stressed in some other way—and have suddenly wanted to be carried like a baby or perhaps even wanted to have a bottle.

The most important change for five year-olds starting regular school is the change in their relationship with parent figures. They are now required to be more independent. This means that the child needs to take on more responsibility for his own needs—in other words become to some small extent his own parent. This process will have been ongoing since birth, but at this point of transition he is faced with a sudden increase in this regard.

It has been shown that young children experience varying degrees of separation anxiety when left by their mother or mother substitute. By the age of five most children are able to cope with separation for part of a day and may have already been doing this in a play group or preschool classes. They may also have been helped to do this by the practice, common in most nursery groups, of encouraging a mother to stay with her child at first, in order to make the separation a gradual process. In this way children have a chance to become a little accustomed to the new setting before being left on their own. There are, however, a number of children who still find this difficult when they start school. Their distress may be expressed openly by crying at the point of separation or may show itself in less obvious ways—they may start waking during the night or perhaps developing tummy-aches and headaches in the morning before school.

In the face of physical symptoms of this kind it can be quite difficult for you as a parent to know how best to respond. Of course you want to take due account of your child's state of health and not to send him or her to school when unwell, and it can be quite difficult to decide whether the headache or tummy-ache might well right itself or not. Undoubtedly you will sometimes get it wrong! However, if you think that these symptoms may be a way of telling you that your child is finding going to school something of a struggle it might help to share your awareness of the fact. You may find that your acknowledgment of this difficulty enables your child to talk about it and help to resolve it. It may also help to talk to the teacher so that she or he too is aware of the difficulty as well as perhaps being able to share with you his or her experience of your child at school. The teacher may have noticed signs of difficulty or, alternatively, may be able to reassure you.

There are many different ways that children have of meeting the new demands of independence that they face at this time. Some children revert to earlier behavior patterns and perhaps demand more attention and babying at home, as if to reassure themselves that they have not lost their parent, while others can react by behaving very independently and taking every opportunity to demonstrate a capacity to cope—like Sally who insisted on walking to school alone, to the consternation of her older sister who was expecting to walk with her! This was Sally's way of managing her feelings of vulnerability, attempting to convince herself that she was able to cope despite some inner feelings of doubt.

Preparation for starting school

Before starting school most children will have heard people around them talking about it. They may have a brother or a sister already at school, or if not they will be aware of other children going to school, and will no doubt be very curious to find out more. They will probably have become aware of the great importance that is attached to it. One often hears children in nursery groups talking animatedly about going to "big school."

Expectations about starting school vary considerably from individual to individual. It will be very helpful for children to have a chance to talk about these expectations before they start school, offering them an opportunity to think about it in more concrete ways and to link this information with their past experience. Opportunities for doing this may present themselves in a number of different ways. For instance, there may be references to school in story books that you read to your child. This could provide an opportunity to learn from their comments some of the ideas of what may be in store, a situation that could enable you to correct any false ideas that they may be harboring.

Choosing clothes before starting school can provide another opportunity to talk about school. It provides an opportunity to discuss why it is a good idea to select garments that can be managed easily, such as shoes with Velcro fastenings or elasticized waistbands on pants and skirts for ease of dressing and undressing.

Another possibility of creating the space to think about starting school is the sharing of your own experience of going to school. This may well arise quite naturally in the course of conversation and children are usually very interested to hear their parents' childhood experiences. It is often difficult for them to believe that adults were ever children like them!

Many schools offer the chance of a day's visit prior to starting, offering an opportunity to taste the experience as it were, enabling children to have something to hold on to in the intervening period before starting.

Preparation of this kind can also help to establish a realistic idea of what's in store. I am reminded of John, who on his return from school on the first day said to his mother, "I've been to school now. What are we going to do tomorrow?" For John the preparation had been inadequate. His ability to understand the concept of continuity was such that he did not appreciate the possible meaning of the statement that he was to go to school as implying a daily event rather than a single visit. This example illustrates the different perception of time that a five year-old has from an adult.

The world of school

All children will have built up certain expectations from previous experiences, particularly those within the family, involving the adults who have been most meaningful in their lives. They will have an idea of how adults are likely to react to them; for example, whether they expect to have to cope on their own. When they arrive in school their view of the teachers is bound to be colored by these expectations. For instance a child might expect that if something is lost the teacher will find it for him, only to be told that children should first try to look for it themselves.

A child from a home where there is a very relaxed attitude about daily routines may find it difficult to respond to a more structured routine in the classroom. Gradually children are able to modify their perceptions as they get to know the teacher and can respond to his or her own characteristics.

The world of school is very different from that of home. The five year-old now finds him or herself one of a group of probably about twenty children and their freedom to please themselves is severely curtailed. At a nursery group they will probably have been able to choose the activity they wish to engage in, while at school they will often be expected to perform tasks within a prescribed range.

In addition, finding yourself a member of a large group of children means acquiring new skills in order to manage. Children of five are still in the process of learning how to play co-operatively—a process which requires the ability to be aware of the needs of others. This can only follow when they have developed sufficient sense of self to feel secure enough to think of the needs of others.

The ability to play co-operatively, therefore, requires a considerable degree of maturity. If we look closely at five year-olds playing what may seem like a co-operative game, closer inspection may reveal two children involved in an activity largely determined by one of the pair, who is instructing the playmate in every detail of the game. Where a more passive child finds some satisfaction in the game, the game may continue, but often it will finish when there is no longer enjoyment in the role he or she has been cast in. A good deal of negotiation is required for a truly cooperative game with an awareness and acceptance of the other person's needs as well as one's own—a process that requires some ability to tolerate frustration.

The following observation is an example from a kindergarten class.

Two little boys were playing with a train set. They were busy constructing the rails, each adding bits independently. One of them then began to build a separate track but his playmate objected and told him to put it elsewhere. He did not protest and did as he was told. He then continued to play with his train in his own way but once again was told to do it differently by his playmate and once again he complied. The only point at which he asserted his wishes was when his companion crashed into his train. He then objected, saying, "You're not allowed to crash." These two little boys were not engaged in a mutual game of sharing, they were at this stage still unable sufficiently to accommodate each other's needs.

Forming new relationships

The relationship between mother and infant is an intimate one, beginning from birth with a total dependence on the part of the baby and slowly developing into a relationship between two separate people. The nature of this intimacy and dependence is still quite intense at the age of five and there are likely to be strong feelings around such issues as eating and toileting. It is not at all uncommon for a child in the early days at school to go to considerable lengths to avoid having a bowel movement while in school, feeling somehow too insecure in this new setting.

Children may also find that staying for lunch at school involves coping with some difficult emotional areas. They develop a variety of attitudes towards food; for example the way the food is prepared at home by Mother becomes very important. What seems like the same meal to you or me may seem strange and unacceptable to the child because it is different in some small way from that which he or she is used to. Alternatively children may have many fads about the food they eat. For some children these difficulties may be fairly easily overcome, while for others it may be an area in which they are still struggling to grow. In addition, children may find the impersonal routine of school lunches very stressful. They are required to operate at a fairly high level of independence, managing the actual feeding process as well as learning the routines that operate in their particular school. They also have to cope with different adults caring for them during the lunch hour, who have different expectations again and who are not in a position to get to know the children very well. When possible it might be helpful to allow the child who is having difficulty in managing this situation not to stay for school lunch until sufficiently matured to cope successfully.

Entering school provides children with the opportunity to extend their knowledge of the range of relationships. The relationship that develops with a teacher has some similarities with the relationship with Mother but also some important differences. The relationship with a teacher at this age has a degree of closeness that could be compared with a mother/child relationship-but also has an element of detachment that allows for new experiences for the child.

It is the usual practice in most schools to organize the class groups so that children of this age are taught mainly by one person. This is a reflection of the five year-old's need to have a teacher who can take the place of a parent, in the sense of offering continuity of care. It is more possible with this arrangement for the teacher to know all the children quite well.

This need was very clearly demonstrated for the mother of Pamela. She became very concerned when Pamela, who had settled happily in school during her first term, seemed tearful and unhappy about going to school. Her mother was puzzled by Pamela's account of her school day which consisted of a list of lessons with different teachers. She went to speak to the teacher and was told that the staff had been advised to try teaching the children language and number work separately so therefore they had different teachers. For Pamela this meant that the day was divided into periods spent with three different teachers. Mother learned that other children were also expressing unhappiness and shortly afterwards it was decided to revert to the previous system whereby the children stayed primarily with one teacher. The difference in Pamela was very noticeable as soon as she once more felt secure with only one adult to relate to.

The child's experience of school

In thinking about the impact of starting school it is important also to remember the excitement and interest that a child can experience. Five year-olds are becoming daily more interested in the world around them and at school they are presented with a welter of new information and experiences.

How does the five year-old cope with this challenge? In the first instance it might be noted that it is not an uncommon experience for parents to find that for a while after starting school children are very tired—sometimes even falling asleep over their meal on their return home! This does not seem surprising in the light of the effort required.

It nevertheless remains the case that most children do succeed in coping with the situation. They depend a great deal on their teacher who will become for them a very important person in their life. I referred earlier to the expectations that children build up in the early years, of the ways in which adults are likely to respond to them. These will largely be based on their relationships with their parents or parent substitutes in those early years. At the age of five children are not yet able to function autonomously—they need a parent figure, someone who is sufficiently mindful of their needs and is there to offer support when the task confronted is proving rather difficult, be it a disagreement with another child or a powerful feeling of frustration or even great pleasure. They need to feel that none of these situations will get out of hand, leaving them with a feeling of helplessness either about how to manage a powerful feeling or how to cope with a difficult situation. There is still a need for the teacher to remind children to put their coats on before going outside, to sort out disagreements and to listen and share in feelings of great satisfaction at some achievement.

It is clearly a great help if a teacher can be aware of a child's enthusiasm for a current topic of learning as well as a lack of interest in another. You will no doubt recognize from the foregoing the sort of awareness that you yourself have of your own child, and realize that it is inevitable that the teacher will sometimes need to take on a parental role. One can see clear evidence of this in the universal experience of kindergarten teachers who become aware of being referred to as "Mommy" by children, who then look rather self-conscious when they realize their mistake!

Integrating the world of home and school

The child is now faced with a need to integrate the experience of two quite different worlds at home and at school. This can lead to some apparently quite perplexing behavior. It can feel like a rebuff when you, as an interested parent, inquire of your child at the end of the school day, "What did you do in school today?" to receive the reply, "Nothing!" A number of children deal with the problem of integration by attempting to keep the two worlds apart. Thus one comes across a situation where a teacher and a parent, sharing information, can hardly recognize the child they are discussing as the same one. This can operate in both directions; sometimes the child is an angel at school while he is quite a handful at home and sometimes it is the other way round, there is no problem at home but the teacher is experiencing difficulties.

One of the issues that face children in this situation is a split in loyalty between teacher and parent. They are expected to cope with two quite intense relationships, one at home with parents and one at school with the teacher. How do five year-olds reconcile the different views and, sometimes, values that they hear expressed?

It was difficult for Peter's mother to know how to deal with the situation when Peter came home from school and told her that he had learned that morning that babies only cry to exercise their lungs. She felt that this was a statement that not only lacked evidence but was also a comment that was worrying for Peter in the attitude it expressed about the need to attend to a baby if it cried. It suggested that crying was not a sign of distress and could be ignored. His mother felt that if she contradicted the teacher's statement she might make it difficult for

Peter to trust his teacher, but if she made no comment she would be leaving him to accept what he had been told. In the event she decided to tell him her own views, while also explaining that different points of view were held by different people.

Most parents have at some time been firmly told that they are doing something incorrectly—"My teacher says you should do it like this." Good parent/teacher communication is clearly very helpful so that children can experience a co-operative alliance between these important adults in their life, one in which there is room for parents and teachers to have different ways of doing things while still remaining well disposed towards one another.

The relationship between teacher and parent is important. It can sometimes, however, become complicated by the feelings engendered in you as a parent by the teacher. In the example above, Peter's mother felt angry with the teacher for causing the children unnecessary anxiety and giving what she felt to be incorrect information to the children. Inevitably there will be feelings of rivalry between parents and teachers both acting in a parental role and concerned about the same child. Clearly it is not helpful for your child to experience a relationship with conflict. On the other hand when there is good communication it can be very rewarding to be able to share experiences of your child with a really interested teacher.

Most schools are keen to foster good relations between parents and teachers and usually encourage frequent contact. In recent years there has been an increasing emphasis on parental involvement in the educational process. The importance of the link between home and school, particularly with reference to the relationship between parents and teachers, has been recognized. For example, in some elementary schools parents are invited to help in the classroom in various ways, maybe to help the children cook or sometimes to hear children read. Such arrangements make for greater relaxation in communication between teacher and parent. In addition to the more informal contact all schools have parent-teacher interviews, usually about twice a year. This provides an opportunity for you to discuss your child's progress and development with the teacher.

Choosing a school

What are the factors that you need to consider in choosing a school for your child? It can seem a daunting task to assess what is on offer in any one particular school. Many people base their decision on the reputation of a particular school. A good record of academic success may be one criterion. Another may be based on the observed behavior of the pupils at the school. A further factor might be in terms of the locality of the school and its accessibility from home. Yet another might be whether the children look presentable or wear a school uniform. Still other factors that you might want to consider would be whether the school is a single-sex school or co-educational, whether it is multicultural or it is a denominational school. You may wish to know how many pupils there are in the school and how large the classes are.

It may be worth digressing at this point to consider the question of school uniform. The philosophy that lies behind it is that it creates a feeling of equality among children and gives them a feeling of pride and belonging to the school. It can also be welcomed by a number of parents as it reduces the daily arguments about what clothes a child will wear! Schools not requiring uniforms often have dress codes that students must more or less strictly adhere to. But ordinary street clothes can have their advantages as well. Primary schools encourage children to wear clothes that are easily managed, to make changing for P.E. class easier, especially for young children. This tends to preclude items of clothing such as ties and shirts and blouses with buttons down the front.

So far I have mentioned some of the issues that you might consider in choosing a school for your child. They are all based on what I might call external factors. How might it be possible to consider a broader spectrum of educational targets? This will depend to some extent on your personal point of view of what it is that you hope that your child will get from education. Since the Second World War, education in primary schools has been developed according to the philosophy that it is a process of facilitating a child's total development, both personal and intellectual. Schools vary in the emphasis they afford to different aspects. One of the best ways of discovering whether a particular school is aiming generally for the same goals as yourself is to talk to the principal, whose views will be reflected throughout the running of the school.

It may be that your decision has to be a compromise among several factors such as, for instance, accessibility (which of course carries with it the advantage that your child's friends from school will live nearby and they can play together outside school) and preferred educational methods.

CHAPTER TWO

Your Five Year-Old And The Wider World

Religious and cultural differences

As five year-olds become involved in the world outside, they will inevitably be exposed to different viewpoints and beliefs, particularly those of the different religions and cultures becoming more prevalent in our increasingly multicultural society, and this requires sensitive handling both at home and at school.

How do Jewish or Muslim children experience the Christmas preparations which become an important part of most schools in the period leading up to Christmas? What happens if they start singing the Christmas carols they have heard when they get home? How do they experience the need to eat food which is different from that being eaten by the majority of the children? It is a situation which inevitably highlights differences between people with the resultant comparisons and feelings of rivalry.

In many schools, as well as elsewhere, attempts are made to capitalize on the situation by introducing children to the differences of race and religion that exist, and encouraging them to share different beliefs and customs with each other. Sometimes, for instance, parents of children from an ethnic minority may be invited in to demonstrate how to cook a traditional dish, and attempts made to introduce reading books that include stories about children from other cultures.

How can you as a parent help? If you come from an ethnic minority you will probably want to keep alive much of your own cultural inheritance and pass it on to your children. At the same time they will be exposed to North American culture at school and will need help in integrating the two. It will be of great help to them if you can take an interest in all the new experiences they are having and which indeed you may be sharing. If they sense that you can accommodate both cultures they might avoid the possibility of feeling disloyal to you if they show interest in their new environment.

All parents, whether or not they are from an ethnic minority, can help their child to accept and appreciate the differences between cultures and religions in the same way, by sharing in their child's experience of them and perhaps thereby increasing their own understanding.

The need for rules

Any keen observer of five year-olds will quickly become aware of the concern for rules that is expressed by the children themselves. As soon as any child deviates from a known routine instruction such as, for instance, where lunch boxes are to be placed as children arrive at school in the morning, one or more of the offender's classmates will put him or her right in a tone of some urgency. In the words of an experienced elementary school principal, "If we don't give them rules they'll ask for them!" At the same time there is a growing appreciation of the meaning of rules in games and with it a growing capacity to tolerate losing in a game. Offering a child the opportunity to play games of all kinds is a way of helping a child of this age to develop amongst other skills that of functioning in a group situation. It seems that operating within carefully laid down rules offers a secure framework for a child managing a new and unknown situation.

The degree to which individual children will need to surround themselves with rules will vary according to their particular personality make-up. In some children it can become a marked feature of their behavior, like Jonathan, whose teacher remarked on the fact that his favorite question seemed to be "Am I allowed?" Jonathan's method of coping with the considerable anxiety he experienced in a new situation was to look for "rules" to help him feel safe. Other children, less anxious than Jonathan, will probably feel less need for a set of rules to govern every aspect of their behavior.

On the other hand there are some children who may not yet have developed a sufficient sense of their own identity to be able to hold on to the idea of rules. They are still at the stage of needing a parent figure to supply all the boundaries for them. These are the children who will frequently need to be told and reminded of the rules, rather than being able to "remember" rules for themselves and abide by them.

Rules provide a framework within which to feel safe. Similarly a set way of working, or performing a task according to a carefully laid out plan can also provide a framework that is helpful. The following examples are good illustrations of this.

The first concerns a group of four children in a kindergarten classroom who were playing a game which consisted of building colored towers. Each child in turn threw a die which had a different color on each face. If the color on the die was the correct one, verified by a picture of the completed tower on a card which each child had in front of him, the child could add the bead of that color to his tower. Two girls, Mary and Susan, and two boys, Stephen and Roger, were playing. At first progress was slow. Roger, the oldest of the group, took it upon himself to instruct the others at each move. Mary and Susan accepted his word, as did Stephen at first. As time went on and the more dominant Roger was making little progress, he began to cheat and turned the die to show the color he wanted. None of the other three children seemed to notice this, but at the same time Stephen began to make great progress legitimately. This encouraged Roger to break more rules and he now began to take his turn too soon. Stephen protested that it should be Mary's turn. His previously passive attitude had now gone and his insistence won the day. Mary was allowed to have her turn, followed by Stephen who was waiting eagerly for his, which was next, and once again he managed to add another bead to his tower. Stephen's pleasure in his success was evident. He was oblivious of Roger, who was by now claiming triumphantly that he had won. The correct completion of his tower was more important than the concern about which child finished first in Stephen's mind. He did not show any sign of expecting the other children to acknowledge his success. He did show, however, every sign of great personal satisfaction at the tower he had made that matched the picture.

Another somewhat different example concerns Elizabeth's behavior in the school Christmas play. She had a central role as the fairy on the Christmas tree, which she carried out with great confidence. Some way through the performance Santa Claus came on to the stage. Suddenly Elizabeth ceased to be the fairy, stepped forward and said in a loud whisper, "You're not supposed to be on yet!" Clearly she could cope with the demands of the performance only if the "correct" procedure was adhered to.

Socialization

Most people consider the ability to make friends among peers very important. It establishes us as being part of a wider network in the community outside home. It may be that as parents you try to ensure that your children have friends, possibly by socializing with friends who also have children of the same age. However, friendships at this age tend to be rather transitory. There is no doubt that for five year-olds at school the teacher plays a more significant role for them than the peer group.

Boys and girls of this age often play together, unlike the situation a couple of years later, when on the whole boys and girls tend to play separately. Much has been said and written on the vexed question of differences between boys and girls. Do these exist as a biological fact or are they the result of conditioning by a society riddled with gender stereotypes? It is not the object of this book to enter a discussion of this issue, merely to note that there do seem to be observable differences in the behavior of boys and girls and making friends is one of them. Girls tend to have one or two friends while boys are likely to relate more casually to several others. The five year-old has not yet developed sufficient powers of negotiation and compromise, the necessary ingredients of any relationship between equals, to enable them to form strong friendships. Hence it is very common to hear a little girl of this age loudly telling her friend of yesterday that she won't be her friend any more. This may be the result of some disagreement where there had been no room for compromise and often the disagreement is temporary; in a short time the friendship is restored. Boys of this age may resort to physical aggression in similar circumstances, or seek another playmate for a while. It is a characteristic of girls that they show a greater concern for the opinion and approbation of adults than boys do. It seems as if girls generally feel a need for reassurance about their acceptability that most boys do not require to the same extent.

Rivalry is common at all stages of life, but the areas of greatest competition are a little different for boys and girls. Girls may be heard asserting that their mother or father is superior in some way to their peers'. Boys on the other hand are often very rivalrous with each other, particularly with regard to strength and size or physical prowess. It is not uncommon to hear them vying with each other about how fast they can run or who is taller or who can perform the most difficult feat on the climber.

A note of caution: Although differences such as these between boys and girls are apparent in general, there are bound to be exceptions and all children, like all adults, are unique.

The games of five year-olds

Five year-olds have not yet reached the stage of playing set games where a set of rules is adhered to, such as soccer or tag. Their ability to participate in group games of this kind comes a little later. Instead they may choose to play games involving role play, often based on their favorite TV program, such as Batman, Superman, Power Rangers and others. They are programs featuring characters that can be easily mimicked. Other games might well be variations on playing "Mothers and Fathers" or "Schools." These games reflect a young child's preoccupation with relationships between individuals, a necessary part of the process of growing up and finding out how to relate to others in a variety of settings. Later on they will be able to enjoy taking part in group activities, for which they need to be able to forgo some of their personal wishes in order to conform to those of the whole group.

Children of this age are still developing motor skills and indulge in a lot of physical activity. Most playgrounds offer them the opportunity to climb, swing, jump or slide on apparatus permanently fixed. By the age of six most children will have fully acquired the large motor skills. Their play may vary between vigorous physical activity and the more imaginatively based games referred to earlier.

Girls begin to develop an interest in activities that require finer motor skills, such as skipping and ball games. Along with these go the jingles that form part of the games that pass from generation to generation. You will no doubt remember some of your own favorites from this stage of your life. In addition to these games are the singing games, more often played by girls than boys, that have regional variations but are passed down from generation to generation, albeit with slight alterations.

One example is a game that consists of one child playing the part of Mr. Crocodile while the others stand a little way away facing him/her. They then sing or chant:

> Please Mr. Crocodile
> May we cross the water
> To see your ugly daughter
> Floating on the water
> Like a cup and saucer?

Mr. Crocodile answers, "Only if you're dressed in red [or some other color that she decides on]." The children who fulfill this condition then run to an agreed "home" and Mr. Crocodile tries to catch them. If a player is caught she becomes Mr. Crocodile.

The type of games that we have been considering are those that take place on the whole in a playground. However, it can seem daunting to a small child to be faced with a large playground full of children. There are in this situation few of the clear rules or set procedures referred to earlier that help to make children feel secure. Some deal with this by trying to stay close to the adult on duty in the playground. Others seek out older brothers or sisters if possible and play with them, although it would be helpful to note that it can sometimes be a burden for an older brother or sister to feel obliged to look after a younger sibling.

The discovery of the peer group

As a five year-old settles into this new environment he or she begins to discover some of the pleasures of being a member of a peer group. One expression of this may be the acquisition of a number of pieces of doggerel verse that are learned and relayed with great enthusiasm to parents.

They may not be received by parents with the same enthusiasm!

When Jane came home one day and recited with great pleasure,

> Oo-ah! I lost my bra
> I left my panties
> In the boyfriend's car

her mother was somewhat taken aback. This was something that belonged to Jane's world—the world of her peer group—and did not originate from adults. The rhyme demonstrated an awareness of the possibility of independence, and brought with it feelings of pleasure, part of which was the desire to shock her parents and to experience the power of a new "authority" which came from her peer group.

The concern and interest in the peer group that begins to become more apparent at this age may also show itself also in a challenge to family "rules" that have previously been accepted. Thus parents are confronted by a son or daughter demanding to stay up later than his or her bedtime because another child does. Or a child assures their parent that it is absolutely essential to be provided with some article of clothing that another child possesses.

Children become aware of different forms of speech. They hear another child using a word such as "ain't" which they have not come across before, become intrigued by it and begin to repeat it endlessly. You will certainly recognize several "in" words that your child begins to use once he or she starts school!

Growing interest in the peer group provides an opportunity for the children of different backgrounds to become aware of each other. The experience of kindergarten teachers is that there is very little evidence of racism amongst children at this age.

CHAPTER THREE

Intellectual Development

An important part of school life for your five year-old is the opportunity to learn new skills, develop the capacity to think and to find ways of expressing creativity. No doubt your ambitions for your own child will reflect to some extent your own experiences; maybe you did very well at school yourself and hope that your child will be equally successful. Or it could be that you found learning at school difficult or problematic in some way and hope that your child's experience will be different. You may feel that for your child practical skills are more important than academic achievement. In any case you no doubt hope that he or she will learn the basic skills of reading and writing.

What are the factors that affect a child? What kind of environment will lead to successful learning? There are several important elements involved. The first of these is the level of innate ability. On the one hand it has been widely believed that babies are born with differing levels of ability, genetically inherited from their parents. On the other hand there is a body of opinion that would argue that this is not so, that intellectual aptitude is determined by the external environment alone. It is very difficult to arrive at a scientifically sound conclusion on this subject as both factors inevitably interact, and it becomes extremely difficult to separate them. Attempts to do so have involved studying identical twins (who have the same genetic make-up) who have been separated and brought up by different parents. The evidence from these studies is inconclusive. However, the experience of teachers is that there are differences between children in their ability to learn, which is separate from the interest and effort expended by the child.

Most children when they start school are full of curiosity about everything around them. This is an enormous help to them in the process of learning, for not only do they need some ability but they also need to want to find out. You will probably have already experienced your child bombarding you with questions—"Why?" "What?" "When?"—and they have no doubt already learned a great deal in this way. The spirit of inquiry will be fostered at school as an essential part of the learning process.

Learning to read

Probably the first and most important scholastic skill you will be hoping to see your child acquire is the ability to read. A few children may have acquired the beginnings of this much earlier, although the average child does not start reading until around six years old. How does a child learn to read? It could be looked upon as little short of a miracle!

Nobody has yet been able to explain completely the process any more than we fully understand the process of acquiring language in the first few years of life. It does involve an ability to symbolize, i.e., the ability to understand that letters written on a page represent words, and that a group of words makes up a sentence. Then there is a further process of recognizing the link between spoken language and the written word—that is, appreciating the meaning of what is read. Young children who can read may stumble and fail to read words that make up a phrase that they don't understand. For example, a child may successfully read the sentence, "I can see his face in the darkness," but fail to read the sentence, "Darkness was on the face of the deep."

Your child will probably have had books at home and have listened to stories that have been read to him or her. This will help a great deal in providing the motivation that I mentioned earlier. Now your child will want to be able to read for him or herself, having experienced the pleasure it can give. Learning to read has been shown to be linked with the development of language, so that the child whose language develops slowly often takes longer to learn to read.

Educators do not agree on how to teach reading most successfully. For a long time it was exclusively thought that a child should start by learning the sounds of letters (phonics). Thus readers contained such sentences as, "The cat sat on the mat." This method depends on the principle that it is necessary to learn all the letters of the alphabet and their sounds and from there move on to tackling new words by recognizing the sound of each letter and "building" the word. This approach lays little emphasis on the meaning of what is read and is felt to be limited for that reason. It is also difficult to produce interesting stories with the necessarily limited vocabulary.

There followed a school of thought that believed that children needed to learn to recognize the pattern of letters that make up the word and that it was therefore easier to read texts containing words of differing lengths. Children were taught to recognize a word in its entirety without breaking it down into its constituent parts. This method was called "Look and Say" or "Whole Word." This approach has been criticized because reading books have to build a vocabulary slowly and each book in the series will only be able to use a few words. As with the phonic approach this limits the scope for making a story interesting. It is felt that interest in the subject matter will increase motivation and therefore facilitate learning.

In order to try to address this problem another method that has been tried is one where reading and writing are linked closely together and children are encouraged to write their own sentences with a gradually growing vocabulary. In this way the child is linking spoken language to the written word.

There has been some criticism of the stress that has been laid on the importance of reading books being interesting to a child. The critics maintain that if the teaching of phonics is ignored the child has no way of tackling a new word, which remains necessary at times, even as an adult. It seems that for many children phonic skills need to be taught at some stage but perhaps after the child has acquired an interest in reading and experienced the pleasure of being able to read a little.

Books for young children always have a proportionately large number of illustrations by comparison with the print. This is undoubtedly to increase the ease with which children can understand the content. One of the ways of learning new words is by a process of guessing a word either from the context or from a picture. Thus the first reading books can offer a more interesting story than would be possible, given the very limited vocabulary available, by means of illustrations.

One of the teaching aims is to foster an interest in reading both for pleasure and for information. It is therefore important to take into account variations in taste so that children can choose to read those books which appeal to them most. There is at the same time a pleasure in acquiring the skill of reading for its own sake—a fact that can help a child to persevere with a simple text that perhaps does not appeal a great deal.

Learning to read is not confined to a child's school experience. As a parent you will become aware of your child's interest in reading notices and signs that you come across in daily life. A great deal of this kind of learning takes place during the acquisition of a reading skill and enables you to share the excitement and pleasure children feel when they experience success in their attempts.

Reading stories is not only an act of pleasure, it can also serve a very useful function for children in addressing some of their most primitive fears. Perhaps this is most obvious in fairy tales that feature witches and dragons, fairies and princes. These stories, most of which exist in various forms throughout the world, represent some of the most deep-seated anxieties of mankind and provide a way of coming to terms with them at a symbolic level. You probably remember the fairy or folk stories you heard as a child and doubtless have your own favorites.

The development of mathematical skills

Mathematics is another skill that you will no doubt be hoping your child will acquire. Before they go to school children will have had some experience of using numbers. When your child was a baby you may have counted fingers or toes, or you may have shared out candies with a brother or sister or have counted blocks being placed one on top of the other to make a tower. There are also a number of nursery rhymes involving counting that many children are familiar with, such as "Baa Baa, Black Sheep" and "One, Two, Buckle My Shoe."

Most children, by the time they are five, can count as far as twenty. This means that they know the number names that far. It may not indicate the understanding of one to one correspondence. Thus if asked to say how many objects they can see they may not be able to give the correct answer. The ability for abstract thinking is not very well developed at this stage and so the "idea" of a number may still be difficult for children to grasp. They can understand that they have two candies in their hand and that if you give them two more they will have four but may not be able to tell you the answer to two plus two. It is in fact very difficult for a child of this age to understand the mathematical language of addition and subtraction.

An experiment was carried out with a group of five year-olds who had all been doing basic arithmetic such as $3 + 2 = 5$, and $6 - 3 = 3$. They were asked to represent on a piece of paper the following operation that they were shown. A small number of blocks was put on a table and several were taken away or added. None of the children represented what they saw in the way they had done when doing their arithmetic. Instead they devised ingenious alternative ways of representing what they had seen. One child drew a hand adding blocks to the pile and another drew dashes to show where blocks had been taken away. It is clear that they did not link the mathematical language they had used in their arithmetic with the concrete operation they had witnessed.

There have been a number of changes in the teaching of math in the last twenty years or so. Rather than merely being taught computational skills of addition, subtraction, multiplication and division, children are now taught mathematical concepts. They learn, for example, how to classify objects into sets and how to represent information on a graph. At the same time they will learn the basic computational skills. The ability to add numbers comes earlier than the ability to subtract and some children find the latter quite a difficult concept to grasp. In order to become fully conversant with mathematical ideas it is essential to be capable of abstract thought. This is the ability to conceive of an idea and be able to develop it mentally to provide a solution to a problem.

The development of abstract thinking

Katy had heard that the next-door neighbors were "moving house." She lived in a semi-detached house. On returning home one day she looked at the house and said to her father, "The Brewsters can't move—their house is stuck to ours"! Katy could only understand the expression "moving house" in a concrete way, such that she envisaged the house itself being taken to another place. But in posing the problem to her father, Katy seemed to be demonstrating that there might be an alternative way of understanding what she had heard and the hope that her father might be able to help her to do so.

Intellectual and emotional development proceed side by side throughout childhood. This is nowhere more apparent than in the area of abstract thinking. Five year-olds are still at the stage of largely concrete thinking. They have not yet reached the stage of being able to think through a process mentally to any great extent. This is one of the reasons for the difficulties that have been referred to earlier in terms of a fear of separation. It is not easy for a child at an early stage to hold on to the idea that Mother will return. If they cannot see her they do not yet feel totally secure in the belief of her continued existence. You have probably witnessed at some time the utter panic shown by a young child who suddenly becomes aware of having "lost Mother" in a store. Sometimes if a young child finds the absence of Mother difficult it can help to leave some object belonging to her, which acts as a concrete reminder of her.

By the age of five children have, however, developed some way towards the capacity for abstract thinking and can be greatly helped by an adult helping them to verbalize a process. You as a parent might talk with your child about a proposed outing, or a visit to friends or relatives, thereby rehearsing future events and helping your child to create a mental image for him or herself. Later it becomes less necessary to spell out every detail as children become more able to create the images for themselves.

Language development

Language is a form of communication between people, and as such plays a very important part in our lives. We have seen in the previous section that the ability to read is closely linked with language development. Reading is of no use unless it conveys meaning to the reader. There are also other forms of language, for example mathematical language, which children need to learn.

Most children at five have a good command of their native language, although they still need to develop it further. You will probably be familiar with the situation when your five year-old tries to tell you about a happening at school and you are left wondering exactly what did happen, as the account you have been given is lacking in certain essential details. You can probably recall occasions, particularly at an earlier age, when your child was telling daddy or granny about an event that you were involved with and you were then able to supply the missing details yourself. At this age children find it difficult to put themselves in another's shoes, so to speak, and therefore they make false assumptions about the listener's knowledge.

Helping a child to discover language skills is also an important part of the school curriculum. It is likely that a teacher will encourage verbal communication a great deal both between herself and the children and among the children themselves, and one would not expect a class of five year-olds to be silent except when listening as a group.

So far we have been discussing children from English-speaking families where the native language is English. If your child does not yet speak English the situation at school will be rather different. Many schools now have facilities for teaching English to children whose first language is another tongue. However, it is important to be aware of their level of understanding as they begin to use English. Recent studies have shown that although it might appear that children can converse fluently in English, closer examination reveals that their understanding is limited. It has been found that while it can take up to two years to acquire proficiency in a second language it can take as long as five to seven years to become sufficiently proficient to cope with abstract language. This means that the teacher will need to take care to ensure that the child has really understood what has been said and if necessary "translate" more abstract language into language that can be more easily understood.

It may be that you and your partner have different native languages. Perhaps one of you speaks English and the other a different language. Often a child learns to speak first in the language of the mother, as communication with her in infancy is more frequent. Much of the communication with a baby happens at feeding times or bath times and it is in this way that language begins. Some parents want their children to grow up to be bilingual. It is seen as an advantage to be able to converse fluently in two languages with less effort than is usually required to learn a new language. Studies have shown that coping with two languages at the same time can delay language development. If one language becomes predominant it is found that ability in the other tends to regress. It often means that children taught in English in school retain the ability to speak the second language but may find reading and writing it needs to be learned later. Very often children from bilingual families can understand the second language even if they are unable to speak it.

In the case of bilingual communities, the experience is a little different and children are able to acquire both languages simultaneously.

If children are born severely deaf they will be unable to hear spoken language and therefore do not learn to speak in the way that hearing children do. These children require specialized help to learn to communicate, which they can achieve by means of sign language as well as by learning to lip read. It is a real challenge for deaf children to acquire language skills and means that they do not have the use of words for self expression in the way that hearing children do.

Some children have less severe problems with hearing which can affect their acquisition of language. Partial hearing loss, which can sometimes be caused by the condition called "glue ear," is fairly common in young children. It is a condition that can easily be overlooked and is therefore a possibility worth bearing in mind if you find that your child is accused of not attending to what is being said. Of course this is made more difficult by the fact that sometimes children can "switch off" and ignore you for reasons other than not being able to hear.

Children who have difficulty in learning

Sometimes children do not make the progress in the basic skills outlined above, that you as a parent might have hoped for. There could be a number of reasons for this. Perhaps they are finding settling in particularly difficult and are preoccupied with concerns about that, or perhaps they are one of the children who learn more slowly than others.

There is, however, another group of children who seem to experience specific difficulty in learning to read and write. These children are often intelligent and can converse well, displaying a good grasp of many areas of knowledge. Typically such children may have a poor sense of time. They may seem muddled about the meaning of prepositions such as "after" and "before." Sometimes they are children who find it very difficult to admit that they don't know an answer and might possibly assert that they know, when in fact they don't. This is frequently a method of coping with a strong fear of failure. They are children who seem to find it difficult to be a child and are sometimes described as acting as if they were grown-up. Along with this often goes a powerful wish for independence.

Competition: its place in learning

The children we have been considering in the previous section, who find the role of a child difficult, do so because they feel very competitive with adults, particularly those that are most meaningful to them, their parents and their teachers. All children aspire to be adults and indeed it needs to be so, as this is the spur to growth. For most children this wish goes along with an ability to enjoy the privileges and pleasures of being a dependent child. On the other hand there are some children for whom the longing to be an adult is so strong that they cannot enjoy their childhood as they might and have to find ways of trying to convince themselves that they are not dependent children. For such children these competitive feelings make it difficult for them to learn, as to do so entails an acknowledgment of the adult's superior knowledge. There is no doubt that competitive feelings are very much a part of a human being's existence and can be used either constructively or negatively in a destructive way.

Many people feel that to encourage a competitive attitude among children is a good way of spurring them on to greater efforts and that in the absence of it children will not bother to make any effort. The situation is more complicated than it seems. For able children, who find the tasks they are set well within their grasp, they may relish the knowledge that they are "top of the class" and this might then encourage them to make further efforts. For the children who have greater difficulty in managing, their feeling of failure may make them less enthusiastic to make a great effort when they feel that they rarely experience success.

Educationalists have given a great deal of thought to this subject in order to find the optimal way of enabling all children to succeed to the best of their ability without leaving some with a feeling of having failed. One method that is prevalent in a number of elementary schools is that of encouraging children to measure themselves by their own performance rather than by comparison with others. Thus, children are encouraged to improve on their own performance.

"Nothing succeeds like success." This saying has been amply demonstrated by studies that have shown that students who felt successful at school were able to do better than those children of much the same ability who did not feel successful at school.

Some children may find alternative areas of success. They might for instance find that they are particularly good at physical activity or games. Playing games is, of course, another area where competition plays a large part. As we have seen, children at five are only just beginning to enter this world of competition.

Children themselves inevitably make comparisons with the others in their class and attempts to disguise the differences in intellectual ability always fail. It is true that these differences are part of the world that the children live in and they need gradually to develop a realistic knowledge of themselves and their capabilities. Nevertheless, if the general attitude of the adults suggests that unless a child is successful academically he or she is somehow less valued it is likely that he or she will suffer a damaging loss of self esteem. There is clearly a need for children to experience success and this is an important part of helping them to learn. At the same time it is important for a child to learn to tolerate a certain amount of failure: it is partly through failure that we learn. Provided that success outweighs failure most children will thrive and learn.

Helping children who have difficulty in learning

How can you as a parent help if your child is experiencing difficulty in learning to read? It may seem tempting to spend a lot of time trying to help him or her read. If you have already done this you may have found it a frustrating experience, in common with many other parents in a similar situation. Your eagerness to help may mean that when the child cannot remember the word you had told him only moments earlier for the umpteenth time, you become very frustrated and impatient. The child will probably feel upset at letting you down and miserable at his or her ineptitude. It is a recipe for disaster!

Continuing to read stories, frequently an enjoyable experience for both parent and child, is a way of keeping alive a love of books. It is also helpful to bear in mind that if children have a fear of failure they will be helped by being given tasks in which they succeed. In the case of children who are finding it hard to tolerate being a child and like to adopt an adult role whenever possible, it might be important to make sure that they are not behaving in such an adult way that it is hard to remember that in some aspects of their life they may still feel quite babyish.

It is sometimes the case that such a child may find some particular area of expertise, such as modeling, which does not require any reading skill. Success at this could perhaps lead on to a greater ability to tackle areas of difficulty. The apparently most obvious way of helping—by helping to read—may be the least effective.

It can be very perplexing for you as a parent to experience this, particularly if you have had the experience of another child who has enjoyed your reading along with them and been helped to progress in this way. It does seem the case, however, that for some children, acquiring the skill of reading has become associated with powerful feelings which make the normal process of learning ineffective.

CHAPTER FOUR

Your Child In The Family

The five year-old is continually developing a clearer sense of self, leading to a growing awareness of a world outside home. This not only affects your child but also his or her relationship to the family. As a parent you will no doubt welcome your child making friends with others. However, it can be difficult to know how best to respond if you discover that you do not approve of the behavior the friendship leads to! Balancing the need to encourage the development of the individual along with the need to set standards important to you is often not easy.

As the five year-old becomes more interested in the world outside home it may seem appropriate to encourage them to attend recreational classes such as dancing, judo or gym, or introduce them to learning to play a musical instrument. The choice of these activities can sometimes be as a result of a particular hobby or interest of the parents. Maybe you are keen on dance yourself and believe that it helps a child develop good deportment, or you may enjoy playing a musical instrument yourself, or perhaps can't and wish that you could. Similarly, many fathers who are proficient athletes may be anxious to introduce their son to the skills required to play those games and by the age of five their child can begin to learn them.

While many five year-olds will derive pleasure from the opportunity to develop new skills it is important that in your role as parent you are able to accept the disappointment that you might feel if your child does not share a particular interest that has great value for you. In the event of that happening you will need to help them discover those things that do interest them.

Position in the family

The position of a child within the family can make quite a difference to the way they experience life events. You yourself may have memories of being expected to look after younger brothers or sisters, or perhaps you were afforded privileges if you were the oldest in the family. On the other hand, if you were the youngest perhaps you resented always being treated as the baby, although at times perhaps it also meant that you were singled out for some special treatment. Those children who have a middle position experience possibly a mixture of these; sometimes they are in the position of the older child and sometimes the younger.

The oldest child of the family has a special relationship with their parents. He or she will have had the experience of being the only child with no competing demands from another. In addition the arrival of the first baby is a particularly momentous event for the parents and the first child therefore has a rather special place in their lives. On the other hand the second and subsequent children probably benefit from their mother's greater confidence in child rearing.

As five year-olds become more involved with the world outside, especially if they are the oldest child, they are breaking new ground. The first one in the family to take this step has no example to follow. This can feel exciting but at the same time it can arouse some mixed feelings of jealousy of a younger brother or sister spending time with Mother alone, reactivating some of the feelings that were there when the younger child was born. As a result mothers sometimes find themselves in a dilemma. When a younger child has, for example, been on a shopping trip or similar expedition she may wonder whether it would be better to avoid the possible jealousy of the older child, who was engaged in another activity, by not talking about it. It is likely that such attempts merely serve to complicate the situation, for the younger child may feel a bit guilty at sharing in an outing that must be kept secret. Probably the most helpful way of dealing with the situation is to acknowledge the feelings of both envy and jealousy when they are expressed, while at the same time showing an interest in the older child's activity, thereby demonstrating your continued concern and love.

There may also be differences in the way brothers and sisters behave towards one another when the first child begins to have a life outside the home. Often the younger children, especially if there is only one, miss the older brother or sister and may show real pleasure when they return home. They also may feel envious of the older child being able to have different experiences and be full of curiosity about them.

Becoming part of a wider peer group brings with it an awareness of strengths and limitations by comparison with them, so that for older children they may no longer be in a position of superiority in terms of skills, as they are at home. They may be faced with others who can equal or perhaps surpass them. One way of coming to terms with this may be to enjoy trying to demonstrate their superiority at home with a younger brother or sister. This may not be received very kindly by the recipient! It is very common, for instance, for children who have just started school to play at "schools" with brothers and sisters. Within the home, where as a rule children feel most secure they may feel able to re-enact situations that have caused them some anxiety from elsewhere, such as school, with brothers or sisters.

Robert was a child who found mixing with a group of children at school difficult. He tended to treat new and strange experiences with great caution as he felt the world to be potentially quite a threatening place. This meant that he had great difficulty in asserting himself with peers and allowed others to dominate him. When he started school he tried to come to terms with this by treating his sister as he experienced being treated at school and he would take her toys away from her and generally tease her much more than he had done before.

For the second and subsequent children the experience of taking the first steps into the outside world is slightly different, as they have the advantage of witnessing their older brother or sister in similar situations. It sometimes happens that older siblings offer advice on managing situations or even come to the younger one's aid at times, providing a source of comfort.

However, unlike the first child who has been used to being more capable than the other children at home, the subsequent children may find that joining a peer group outside the home provides them with an opportunity to discover areas of activity where they are superior to their playmates. This may help them to increase their confidence and go forward, but there are some children who find the feeling of struggling to catch up with an older sibling extremely daunting and they may suffer as a result from a certain lack of confidence in themselves and their abilities.

As a parent you will of course want to help your child to manage these feelings in the most helpful way, so that they can grow and flourish. One way of doing this for the five year-old, feeling his or her way towards self awareness and a knowledge of his or her capabilities, is for you to be aware of the rivalry between siblings, so that he or she does not feel urged to emulate an older brother or sister in a way that might engender a feeling of despair if you have a very sensitive child. It is commonly said that "comparisons are odious" and this is particularly so when thinking about different children in one family.

A situation that usually needs particularly careful handling if it arises is the one when a new baby arrives just at the point that a child is beginning to look outwards at this stage of life. It may give rise to ambivalent feelings about participating in events outside. Your five year-old may feel that if he or she becomes interested in life outside, Mother and Father might turn their attention to the new arrival instead! It will help if you are able to acknowledge those feelings and at the same time take a particular interest in the activities your five year-old has been involved in.

The child in relation to the parents

How do children perceive their parents? One of the ways of learning is by imitation. You no doubt recall how as a baby in a stroller your child would try to imitate your facial expressions such as smiling. A child will not only try to imitate your actions but also your behavior and indeed that is one of the ways of learning how to behave as you would wish. Your five year-old will also be looking at you in your role as an adult and as a parent as part of the process of growing up.

Girls are likely to identify with their mothers, imagining themselves in that role, while boys are more likely to identify with their father for similar reasons. Boys of this age are often preoccupied with proving how powerful they are and games of fictional strong men or creatures are very common, as is vying with one another over who is the strongest or most powerful.

Girls enjoy playing "House" and "Mothers and Fathers" and the five year-old often enjoys playing with dolls caring for them as "babies." It is not uncommon for boys of this age to enjoy playing with dolls too.

Parents tend to be idealized by children of this age. They are seen as the ultimate authority in most aspects of the child's life. It can come as a shock to five year-olds to discover that Mother or Father does not know an answer to one of their questions. It feels too unsafe at this age to tolerate such uncertainty. Pauline could recall many years later the shock she experienced when she asked her mother to tell her whether there was a God. Her parents were agnostic and Pauline had not heard talk of God at home. When she heard mention of it in school she wanted to understand and felt sure that her mother would supply the answer.

Her mother's response was that there were different views on the subject. Some people believed that there was a God and some believed that there wasn't. Pauline experienced a feeling of considerable shock that her mother could not give a definitive answer and the impact of that incident was sufficiently great that it stayed with her for many years.

Working parents

It may be that as a parent of a five year-old who is becoming a little more independent, new possibilities are open to you, such as taking a job or perhaps extending it if you have already been working. It can be very helpful to your child if you are able to fulfill other parts of yourself besides that of parenting. It is another step towards the necessary separation that comes with maturity.

How can you ensure that both you and your child benefit? We saw earlier that young children have a limited capacity to hold all their needs in mind and require an adult to help in this process. Just as it is important to communicate with the teacher to provide a bridging between home and school it is equally important that your child experiences a continuity with you when you meet again at the end of the day. This can be done by taking an interest in whatever communications are forthcoming. In other words it is important to focus your attention on the child's interests and "switch off" from the preoccupations of your day. It is likely that you will know your own child well enough to sense if his or her mood suggests that all is not well. Equally you will be able to join in any expression of pleasure or satisfaction with the day's events.

We spoke earlier of the fragile nature of the child's capacity at this stage to hold on to mental images and the consequent fear of loss. It will help your child to build confidence in your continuing care and concern if you are reliably there as arranged, to pick him or her up at home time.

Choosing a babysitter

You may already have childcare plans in place but if you now need to arrange for a babysitter to care for your child what are the important points to bear in mind? As we discussed with regard to the teacher, whoever you employ will be parenting your child during the period that he or she is in their care. We have seen that growing up is a process of making sense of the world emotionally and intellectually, a process that is facilitated by consistency of experience. It therefore would be helpful to your child if there was basic agreement between you and a sitter about ways of responding to the child's needs, and it would be important to explore this before going ahead with the arrangements.

What are the most important areas to explore with a potential babysitter? You will want to ensure that you have similar ideas on behavior. For example, it might be very difficult for a child to cope with quite different expectations from your own about the need for being tidy. If you adopt a fairly relaxed attitude to toys lying around while children are playing and can tolerate them making themselves quite dirty and messy at times it will be very confusing if the sitter likes her house to be kept neat and tidy at all times and expects children always to be neat and clean. There may be minor differences in the expectations for clearing up at the end of play or variations in the play materials that either you or the babysitter are prepared to tolerate such as water, plasticine or sand. Another area that is likely to be important is that of food. Attitudes about the wisdom of making children finish all the food on their plate need to be the same, otherwise you are likely to create considerable difficulties for the child in an important area of their life. It would also be difficult for them to accommodate to a very different diet than the one they are used to at home. For instance a change from bland to spicy foods or vice versa may be asking more than a young child can manage, as well as leading to difficulties for the babysitter who may be upset at the rejection of her food. In addition you may have different views on how many treats should be allowed, an area that could prove a problem to your child if the differences are too great.

In looking for a babysitter the most important thing to be aware of is an attitude towards childcare that is similar to your own. It could be tempting to think that you might find a babysitter who was different from yourself and might compensate for some of your own weaknesses. An attempt to do this will probably only confuse your child! Finally, as with the teacher, it would be very important to maintain communication with the babysitter so that you can then help your child to integrate the different experiences.

Managing change

We have seen so far that five year-olds have a growing but tenuous sense of themselves and their place in the world. It does not therefore seem surprising that major changes in their lives will need careful handling. One such happening might be a house move.

Moving house is a major event for adults. It usually requires a reorientation of many of your daily routines, as well as adjusting to new surroundings both inside the house and outside in the neighborhood. For a young child these adjustments can seem very daunting. Many parents find that even when they go on a holiday young children can find bedtime difficult for the first few nights and they may have problems in getting to sleep. Indeed it is not uncommon for adults to find difficulty sleeping in a "strange bed."

I am reminded of Ian, a five year-old, who was on vacation with his family. He had brought his Lego set with him, and every night in bed before going to sleep he made a house. On his return home at the end of the holiday he rushed indoors and upstairs to the bathroom. His puzzled parents asked what he was doing and he explained that he was sure the bathtub was different. He was certain that it had changed color. It was difficult to convince him otherwise. It seemed likely that the house he made with his Lego every night was a way of trying to keep hold of the image of his house, and his concern to reassure himself that it still existed as he knew it was very evident on his return.

If a temporary absence can arouse such feelings it is reasonable to suppose that a permanent move will also give rise to similar feelings of loss, as well as adjustments to new situations. For example, just as can be the case on holiday, sleeping in a different room can be quite a difficult adjustment for a child of this age. Night time is often the time when underlying anxieties surface. It is a time when separateness is felt acutely. The state of sleep is one where the rational thoughts of consciousness tend to be temporarily lost and irrational and sometimes frightening thoughts take over.

There are of course big changes to cope with in everyday life.

Children, like adults, will need to adjust to their new surroundings both inside and outside the home. They will miss the friends they used to play with. How best to ease this transition? In the same way as we talked about preparation for starting school, talking to a child about the impending change can help to create some idea of what to expect. Taking the child to see the new house when it has been decided on will enable him or her to have a concrete idea about it. It might be helpful here to consider the balance needed in terms of sharing information with a five year-old. You might think that it could be helpful to take them house-hunting and let them share in the decision making in this way. This, however, is likely to make a child very anxious, as they will probably find the uncertainty involved in this process too difficult to cope with. It is better to wait until the decision has been made so that it is possible to share facts rather than possibilities.

Moving will probably involve a change of school as well. Clearly for a child in the first year at school, this is almost certain to be somewhat stressful. It is important that the child is able to acknowledge the leaving in some way. This may simply be by saying goodbye to the teacher and friends. It may be possible to take away some reminder of the experience at school, in the form of some picture or model that has been created there. Hopefully it will have been possible to visit the new school prior to the move so that the child has some idea in mind of what is in store.

The child's place in his family

As part of his growing awareness of his identity, the five year-old shows a great interest in his family and its roots. He wants to understand how he fits in and how the extended family of aunts, uncles, cousins, grandparents are part of where he belongs. Looking at family photographs is a way of sharing some of this information and is an activity that all the family can enjoy. In addition there will have been visits to relatives at various times, which will have provided an opportunity to explain family relationships. No doubt the comparisons that are made between various members of the family help to create a feeling of identity and belonging.

This feature, however, is more complicated for a family with adopted children. If you are an adoptive parent it may be a source of some regret that you cannot attribute personality traits in your child to genetic inheritance within your family. On the other hand, of course, it could be a relief if a particular trait is not very appealing!

If your children are adopted you are also faced with the question of how to handle the communication of this knowledge to them. Parents are commonly advised these days to be open about the fact that a child is adopted from the beginning, so that as soon as the opportunity arises parents are advised to talk about it. It is likely therefore that by the time a child reaches the age of five you will have already had a chance to share the fact that he or she is adopted.

At the time of enrolling a child at school you may be required to produce a birth certificate. This could present you with another opportunity to talk about this and explain further the process of adoption, enabling you to convey that although you are not the birth parents your commitment to your child is the same as if you were and that he or she belongs to your family now.

So far we have considered the five year-old's experiences of various aspects of his life largely from the standpoint of a child who is part of a nuclear family consisting of a mother, father and maybe brothers and sisters. For some children however this is not their experience. Instead, a child may live with only one parent, either because the parents are separated or divorced or one parent has died, or the parents have never lived together. In a previous section we have considered the mutual effects of children meeting others from different racial and cultural backgrounds. In the same way they will discover that family experiences can differ. The child from a two parent family is made aware of the fact that some parents do split up. As there are bound to be times when every child feels jealous of the close relationship between his parents from which he is excluded, this will probably make him feel a little anxious. He may talk about it to you, becoming acutely interested in the subject, in an effort to seek reassurance.

For children from a single parent family it may be a source of concern that they feel different from their fellows. They may well want to know what has become of their second parent and it would be helpful to be able to share this information with them.

If they are the children of divorced parents and spend part of their time with one and part of the time with the other it will be important to inform the teacher at school. This is another situation where there might perhaps be different expectations of the child. It would be very easy for a teacher who was unaware of the situation to enable a child to play off one against the other unwittingly.

The other difficulty that children of divorced or separated parents have to manage is the split loyalty they may feel. We earlier mentioned the split loyalty between the teacher and parent. It is perhaps more difficult to help them when they feel torn between two parents. An awareness of this issue on the part of the adults caring for a young child is the first step towards avoiding it as far as possible, where the parents' concern for the children can help them to present as united a front as possible.

When a single parent who has the care of the children marries or remarries the children and adults have to find a way of adjusting to this new situation. It is perhaps easier for a young child to adapt to a new parent in these circumstances than it is for an older child who has gained more independence and may have had a close relationship with the original parent. For a five year-old, who, as we have seen, still has to work quite hard to understand and manage change, it will probably present quite a challenge, as it almost certainly will to you as parents and step-parents. It requires a good deal of sensitivity

on your part as parents to appreciate the inevitable feelings of torn loyalties as well as the feeling of jealousy about the new parental relationship. It may help if the new partner can find some common interest with the child, but also allowing the relationship to develop at its own pace so that the child can be helped to accept the authority of the new parent in a manageable way.

Looking to the future

We have seen that the five year-old is at a stage of transition in development. In the first years after birth, children have to come to terms with the world they have been born into and cope with many powerful feelings that are aroused in them in their struggle towards maturity. There is a marked spurt in development between five and six and you may be surprised at the changes that occur in your child during the year. Around the age of six or seven this process reaches a point where a reasonable degree of emotional stability has been achieved, so that children are able to turn their attention more fully to the outside world rather than being preoccupied with their inner world.

The stage that follows is one of rapid intellectual growth, the period when children become interested in the world around them and enjoy finding out how things work, while at the same time they make great strides in acquiring general knowledge. This is the period preceding puberty and adolescence, a time when once again the growing child faces a period of emotional turmoil as he or she enters the transition to adulthood. At that time many of the emotional issues that were faced in the early years are re-awakened and there is, as it were, a second chance to resolve some of the areas of difficulty that were perhaps left unresolved at the earliest stage of development.

I have attempted to examine some of the issues around taking the first major steps into the outside world including starting regular school, where five year-olds begin a process of discovery about themselves and their place in the world, a process that can be exciting, fulfilling and sometimes hard work. In attempting to understand your own child's experiences of this process you as the parent are providing the most valuable asset you can give your child on the road to maturity.

FURTHER READING

Early Childhood Education, Tina Bruce, Hodder & Stoughton, London, 1987

Children's Minds, Margaret Donaldson, Fontana, 1978 (For a critique of Piaget's theory of intellectual development)

Human Development: An Introduction to the Psycho-Dynamics of Growth, Maturity and Ageing, Eric Rayner, Allen & Unwin, London, 1978

Narratives of Love and Loss: Studies in Modern Children's Fiction, Margaret and Michael Rustin, Verso, London, 1987

The Author

Lesley Holditch is a child psychologist working in the Child and Family Department of the Tavistock Clinic, where her responsibilities include clinical work and liaison with schools, as well as being a tutor to the postgraduate training course in Educational Psychology. After graduating from London University with a degree in Psychology she taught primary school children and then trained as an educational psychologist, followed by a number of years working as a local authority educational psychologist. Her publications include "Bridge building between teachers and social workers" in *The Family and the School* (edited by Emilia Dowling and Elsie Osborne), Routledge and Kegan Paul, 1986.

Lesley Holditch is married and is the mother of two children who are now grown up.

Understanding Your Child
Titles in This Series

Understanding Your Baby	by Lisa Miller
Understanding Your 1 Year-Old	by Deborah Steiner
Understanding Your 2 Year-Old	by Susan Reid
Understanding Your 3 Year-Old	by Judith Trowell
Understanding Your 4 Year-Old	by Lisa Miller
Understanding Your 5 Year-Old	by Lesley Holditch
Understanding Your 6 Year-Old	by Deborah Steiner
Understanding Your 7 Year-Old	by Elsie Osborne
Understanding Your 8 Year-Old	by Lisa Miller
Understanding Your 9 Year-Old	by Dora Lush
Understanding Your 10 Year-Old	by Jonathan Bradley
Understanding Your 11 Year-Old	by Eileen Orford
Understanding Your 12-14 Year-Olds	by Margot Waddell
Understanding Your 15-17 Year-Olds	by Jonathan Bradley & Hélène Dubinsky
Understanding Your 18-20 Year-Olds	by Gianna Williams
Understanding Your Handicapped Child	by Valerie Sinason

Price per volume: $8.95 + $2.00 for shipping and handling

Please send your name, address and total amount to:

Warwick Publishing Inc.
388 King Street West • Suite 111
Toronto, Ontario M5V 1K2

PAR

~~155.42~~ 649.123
HOL   Holditch, Lesley
       Understanding Your 5 Year-Old

SEP 9 9 ENT'D

ADO 2499

SAND LAKE TOWN LIBRARY
3 1744 00046 5563

Property Of:
Sand Lake Town Library
8428 Miller Hill Road
Averill Park, NY 12018

GAYLORD M